THE GRIEVING TIME

THE GRIEVING TIME

A Year's Account of Recovery from Loss

By Anne M. Brooks

Illustrated by Ted Ramsey

The Dial Press
Doubleday & Company, Inc.
Garden City, New York

1985

Library of Congress Cataloging in Publication Data

Brooks, Anne M., 1919-
 The grieving time.

  1. Bereavement—Psychological aspects. 2. Grief.
I. Title.
BF575.G7B755   1985   155.9'37   84-26069
ISBN 0-385-19801-9

Published by The Dial Press
Copyright © 1985 by Anne M. Brooks
FIRST PRINTING

DEDICATION

To my husband, Bud, and to the grandchildren
he so loved: Annie, Jaimie, Kris, Collin, Seth,
Peter, Samantha, Susannah and Tim.

PREFACE

THE GRIEVING TIME was written as a once a month journal for the year following my husband's death of cancer at 64. The writing is spontaneous and emotional. Beginning the journal as an answer to my need, I grew to realize its value as a therapeutic tool. Every time I wrote or reread it, there was the comfort of releasing sublimated grief.

Nowhere in book stores or libraries could I find any other such help. Sentimental poetry, clinical aids, religious tracts, rather long autobiographies, yes, but nothing that moved me to that needed comfort.

I hope that readers, too, will feel that the depth of their personal grief is real, it is honest, and they are not alone.

ACKNOWLEDGEMENTS

This book never would have been published without the support of my family. My eternal thanks to son Rick, who gave countless hours to assure its publication and success; to his wife, Sarah, who helped all along the way. I wouldn't have even dreamed of publishing it without daughter Patti's urging, and could not have finished it without the encouragement and editing efforts of daughters Cath, Barb, son-in-law Dave Wood and my sister, Helen Morris. Gerri Hirshey gave me the boost I first needed; daughter Penny and her husband Mike kept me going.

Ted Ramsey's drawings, powerful and sensitive, reinforce the emotion in the book in a tremendously personal way.

My thanks, too, to Carolyn Livoy and Nancy Lynch of Delapeake for their willingness to stick with it, and especially to Paul Miles, whose hard work and persistence brought all these elements together.

THE FIRST MONTH

*T*he first few days I feel as though I am sitting in a tree somewhere, watching myself perform. I try to do all the right things —the greetings to relatives, the thank-yous, the speech at the service, more thank-yous, more smiles, more greetings. I am outside myself —as if I have switched off my feelings.

Except that suddenly right in the middle of a conversation, a wave of reality washes over me and I have to leave, quickly, to hide somewhere. I have to hold on to something when it happens — a pillow, the refrigerator, one of his shirts — because of the terrible pain in my chest. Is it my heart? If I think of him, I have genuine waves of feeling sick as well as the pain.

At first I tried not to think of him; it hurt too much. Then as the days go by that's all I do but it's thinking only of the long illness and especially the terrible last three weeks. I think of the special things he said, "What would I do without you? Let me feel your hair."

I am so glad I insisted someone sit with him every minute the last two weeks. Every time he opened his eyes, he would look to see if we were there beside him, and we were. He let us hold his hand all night. There was so much love in the room he must have been comforted.

I hope, oh so much, that although he was unconscious, that somehow he knew when I crawled into bed with him and lay alone with him in my arms as he died.

So much love he took with him.

After all the family leaves, the silence is overwhelming. I try not to think, keep frantically busy — lawyers, the bank, letters to write all day.

The best, the only good time of all twenty-four hours is when I first get into my single bed at night — I have never gone back to the big bed. I am dead, bone-aching tired, but just as I turn over on my side and start to cry quietly, clutching his blue denim shirt in a ball to me, a slow, warm, comforting feeling comes over me. A presence so loving, so comforting. Is it him? It must be.

THE SECOND MONTH

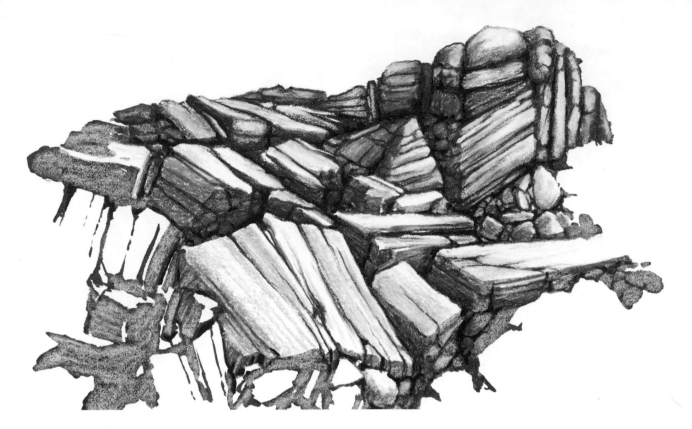

Why can't I dream of him? It is the second month and I simply cannot visualize his face or form. I stare at his picture and can feel my hand on his cheek, or smoothing down hair, but as soon as I put down the picture, he's gone. I try and try. I long to see him, but I dare not look at snapshots or home movies. I will be torn apart.

I would never have believed the physical side of grief. I do feel torn apart. Does this come first, or after the numbness which is its other half of each day? There seems to be nothing in between.

That's not altogether true. A little while each day, I seem to be functioning, mechanically, but still it is a semblance of living. No, not living, existing.

I don't like anything. Not food, not friends, not music.

I love the children, the grown-up ones and the grandchildren. They are my only comfort. They all try so hard to help me, but I am in a world apart even from them. I am surprised at the depth of their feelings, their own grief. They cannot possibly feel as badly as I do; their grief is different. I am wrapped in self-absorption, denying it is self pity. I find faults in all my friends. Why did I ever like them?

Something must be done. I will not be a whining, self-pitying widow. I go to the

*library and check out every book on
grief and widowhood. I finally read all
the pamphlets my daughter has sent.*

*I realize that part of my problem is I
cannot really share any of my feeling
with anyone unless I feel they have
recently gone through the same
experience. So I bridge social chasms
and call up one woman whose husband
is dying and another whose husband
has just died. I don't even know them,
but I stumble through an explanation —
maybe I can help them while they help
me.*

*We do meet, and talk, and it is a help
to me. I feel useful, besides. This is a
good move. I'll do it again.*

*I have lost twelve pounds and
everyone notices. It's not only because
I'm not liking food, it's my frenetic
activity and sleepless nights. I'll sleep
well a few nights and then two in a row
I'll lie there hour after hour, hating my
life, wishing I could turn the clock back.*

*I have not gone through all the states
mentioned in the books and pamphlets.
I've never felt guilty, because all our
lives we knew we had the best there was,
and we tried to appreciate every
moment. Then, too, I tried so hard to
give him everything I had these last two
years. The way he died, too, in my arms
—no guilt there. It was the way it
should be.*

*Not even anger. Having been so close
the whole time, the end seemed
inevitable. Inexorable. At the very end,
he wanted "out" so much, I could not
dream of trying to keep him.*

THE THIRD MONTH

I am finally dreaming of him! It is such
a comfort, so natural. At first, he was
only a shadowy figure, a presence, but
now he is there!

The practical aspects of living creep
up on me. All the business affairs take
up time and I prefer them — nothing
personal to cope with.

The social part of my life is exactly
what the books and articles say. Many
old friends have disappeared into the
woodwork. Never call, never invite me,
seem embarrassed when we meet. I make

special efforts to talk about him
naturally, to ease their embarrassment.
Some doors have just shut, I guess, so
I'll have to find others.

But some friends remain — I
appreciate their every gesture. New
friends who never knew him appear and
I am pleased to be accepted. Maybe I am
a person without him, although I only
feel like a half.

Large parties are deadly. He isn't
there for the entrance or leave-taking.
I no longer have him to gravitate toward

when I'm bored or feeling uncertain. I know these feelings are not so important: they will ease with time.

People keep saying, "It all will get better." The strange thing is I'm not sure I want it to. My grief, the terrible longings, all the agony, are what seem to hold me still close to him. When I cry or rock myself in misery, I feel him near and even call his name.

I am completely asexual (another thing the books say), but there are strange sensual reactions. I hate to take a shower — I am reminded so much how much he loved me. I look at my hands or even my feet and think those are the hands and feet he loved so much. My clothes are all associated with him. I hate them.

The longing to be held, to put my cheek against his, to dance with him is unbearable. I dance one afternoon by myself in the kitchen, tears streaming down my face as the radio plays swing music.

Whatever shall I do?

THE FOURTH MONTH

I'm fine.
    People keep asking, I keep answering, I'm fine. I'm fine.

I smile. I walk briskly. I manage the business affairs extremely well. I go to the few parties to which I'm invited. I smile. I even laugh. I'm fine.

And then when I drive over the bay bridge I don't dare take my eyes off the pavement or I'll see a sailboat, or even just white caps, and I'll burst into tears. But only if I'm alone.

That's the key word. Alone. Dreading it, avoiding it, but needing it. Needing time to be alone to grieve, to cry. And I really mean to cry — loudly, when no one can hear me. Except him, I hope. Time alone when I lean my head against the back door window and cry because the sunset is so beautiful and I almost called, "Come see how beautiful it is!" to someone who isn't there.

Time to be alone, to learn to steel myself to the idea of years ahead. Not just the days I'm barely able to manage, nor the months I dread, but maybe years. Years of no sharing thoughts, or dreams, nor any beautiful things, no special moments, no joy.

Years of looking at the house and the things in the house, every single thing in it meaning something about him. He bought it. He fixed it. He painted it.

He made it. We found it. Nowhere can I look but what he's there. I can't put a log on the fire without seeing him kneel on one knee and do the same.

I can't bear to go in the bedroom where we spent all the nights of loving. All the mornings of lying curled together as though we would never part.

I never dreamed we would. Even the months he was so sick, I kept denying the reality. I kept feeling it was a bad dream. Of course, he'd get better. Of course, he'd never go.

I'm suddenly angry now. Angry that any of it happened. He tried so hard to get better. We fought together. Nights before we went to sleep, we always touched each other's hand. Lots of times we even said the words, "We'll fight it."

And the first one awake in the morning slid over to the other right away. We'd hold on for dear life — so glad we were both still curled up together.

They say it is only the possibility of committing suicide that keeps grief-stricken people from going mad. It's absolutely true. In the moments of terrible total despair, there has to be an alternative to those awful words that haunt —
Forever
Never again
Alone
I'm fine.

THE FIFTH MONTH

I feel as though I am acting in a play and suddenly, at the beginning of the last act, someone has changed the script. I hate the play now ... although I loved it before; but I have to keep on playing my part although it is all wrong for me. I have to think of the rest of the cast and the audience, but I long for the curtain to fall ... to free me from the acting.

People look at me so warily. Is she going to cry if we mention his name? So of course they never do. I, and the children, are the only ones who do. It is easier to do now, but easier doesn't mean easy.

There is no question in my mind that the degree of grief one feels is in direct proportion to the depth of feeling one had before the loss. Everyone feels the separation, some more than others. Some feel anger, some guilt, some fear, some frustration.

But real grief, the kind that shakes your whole being and feels as though you cannot possibly bear it, that is grief, not just loss.

I remember parts of old hymns: "Oh love that will not let me go" — "Remember me." These bits and pieces are the only solace I have found in religion. I don't really believe in heaven, but I do believe he is somewhere. That belief is the thin thread that holds my sanity, the thought that perhaps,

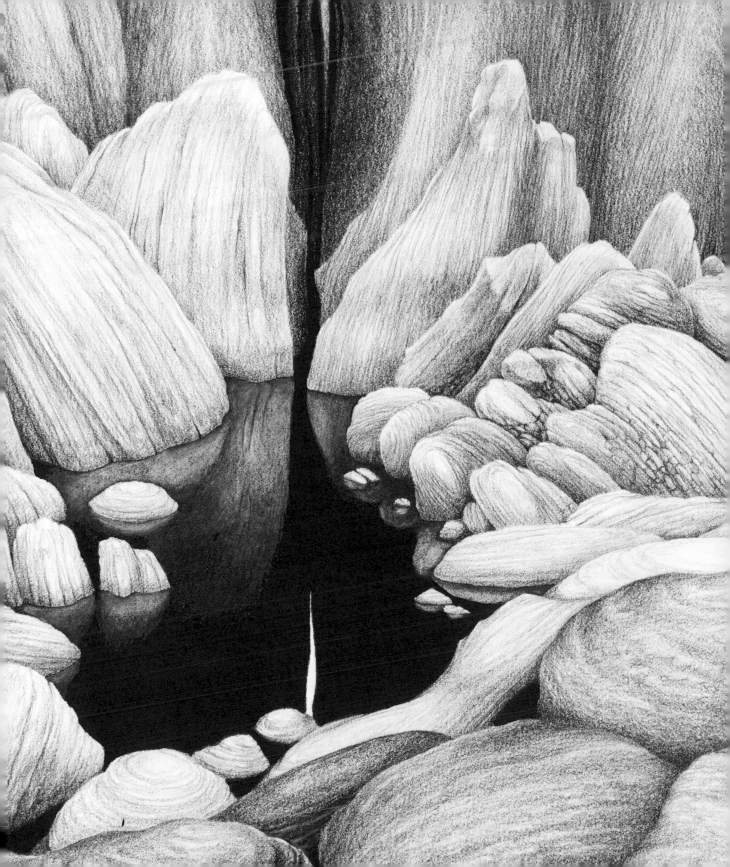

someday, somehow, I will be with him again. This is half the magnetism drawing me to suicide; the other half is simply that life is too unbearable without him.

I have come a long way in five months. For so long, the thought of suicide was lurking behind every move. The promises I had given him deterred me more than anything. Then came emergencies; I really was needed with the new baby, with other problems. I think of what he said to me when we talked about it, "Think of what it would do to the children." Now suicide is relegated to the future; it is my alternative, not my consuming desire.

When the children and grandchildren are around, I realize how far I have come; I come alive. I can talk about him, think about him, laugh about memories with them, all without pain. I still cannot do this when I'm alone.

The spaces of coping and not coping have finally reversed. Most of the time I really am not fine, but not so bad. The good days are more frequent than the difficult ones now, although the pain, when it comes, is still as intense.

Perhaps all the positive moves I made have paid off; the reaching out to other widows, all the reading, the talking to the children. I have forced myself to express my thoughts. Some sort of creative activity, painting, photography, sewing, knitting — anything that makes me feel that I have passed the time productively —is therapeutic. I think I have reached this point faster than many other grievers because I have tried so hard. I listened to every suggestion, accepted every invitation. I had to, or I never could have survived.

Having some of the children so close, with one daughter staying with me for awhile, has helped more than anything else. Just to feel their arms around me on a particularly bad day saves me. They encourage me in all my ventures, support my every move. I feel like their child, but I need this so much.

I think I will have to buy a dog. I must have something near me I can love, that I can touch, can hug.

I am not yet whole. I never will be whole again; but I guess I will be me.

THE SIXTH MONTH

One of the children has compared what is happening to me to the unfolding of a butterfly. As I reread the journal, I can feel it happening. I was totally wrapped in a cocoon until the fifth month, then the first stirrings of life began. Now in the sixth month, I am almost ready to fly ... a far from beautiful butterfly, but maybe I *can* fly.

I believe that I have been able to compress what would normally take a year or two into these six months by a combination of determination and luck. I had no financial problems, no small children, no real problems except my own grief, so I could devote all my energies toward doing something about that grief.

The actual physical problems of living alone have occupied much of my time. The little jobs, taking out the trash barrels, repairing little things, spending hours and hours on paying bills, fighting computers, settling the estate, making decisions that we once shared, all these I do not with the resentment I have read about, but with sorrow. The bigger jobs, either the children help me or I hire them to be done.

Thank goodness for the routine of living —it is automatic. I eat three meals a day, I go to bed, I get up in the morning — because that is what one does. I try to do something when I have to eat alone. Either I watch the television or read the mail or read a book. Otherwise I find I have consumed the whole meal in five minutes.

I still certainly am not fine. Nor whole, but I am functioning to the best of my limits. The limits define themselves at the strangest times and places. Shopping in a country store and wanting to share a "find" will bring tears to my eyes. "Mack the Knife" on the car radio, one of our favorite dance tunes, kept me crying for miles along a lonely stretch of road. The way my son ran along the station platform to greet me was so much like his father. These things hurt, and hurt painfully.

But what is strangest of all is that, having worked so hard to learn to bear these hurts, I now feel guilty because I do. I am terrified that my thinking less often and less intensely about him will somehow let him slip away.

So now I work to keep his memory alive, to keep him with us. I talk about him all the time, especially to the grandchildren. I tell anecdotes and am almost ready to fix the photo albums and the home movies. Part of this is almost masochistic; if it hurts enough, it keeps him near. Someday I'll be able to remember him and will be comforted, but not yet.

THE SEVENTH MONTH

I cannot imagine what life must be like for those people who have never had, as the younger generation says, "a meaningful relationship." Over the years I became so used to having a connection, a pivot, a tether to security. I came first to someone. With Bud gone I no longer come first to anyone. My children have their own families, and so it should be.

Without that lifeline, I feel like the spaceman in the movie "2001" who was deserted in the void, his arms flapping in slow motion inside his space suit the only sign that he remained alive.

I wonder why I reread so many of the letters friends wrote after Bud died. It took a while before they really gave me comfort—at first they were too painful.

Funny how often that word pain crops up. It is the proper word; it is physical pain still, months and months later. But exorcising that pain with grief and tears seems to be the only antidote.

So I do reread the letters I receive from Bud's former patients and our friends. Often I wonder if I am idealizing him the way so many widows think about their husbands. Then I look at another letter from someone else who loved or admired Bud and I realize that he was something special.

People at the hospital have forwarded a letter from one of Bud's students, a Peruvian he had trained when we were in South America. I could tell that it had taken a long time to write: "Dr. Brooks was, to me, my teacher and also my best friend. Like my father." I remember that short, brown-eyed man following Bud around almost like a shadow. So many people like him, who knew Bud for such a short time but who somehow heard of his death and were moved by it.

The letters are like balm. I'm glad I kept them.

I am two people. I am the one everyone sees and talks to. The one who "looks wonderful," who laughs, who visits, who plays, who looks at birds, who sees the spring, who sees the flowers. I am also the woman who hates the spring, hates the flowers, hates her house, hates her clothes, hates her life, hates herself.

I, the inside I, can't cope. I can't face another year of this flat, flat landscape. I am two-dimensional—the one other people see and the one who feels.

And oh, how I feel!

For months now, when I think of him I abruptly pull down the shades of my mind. I talk about him, about his death, about our life, but I don't allow myself to feel anything until I am alone. And seldom do I allow myself to be alone. It is too devastating. Because then, only then, do I admit to myself that he is really gone and I have to continue on without him.

These black times come most often when I am physically tired—too tired to work any more, too exhausted to read. Then I find myself just sitting, staring, not even dreaming; just wishing. And the wishing is not good.

Suicidal thoughts still hang around. I'd do it in a minute if only the children would let me. They have me boxed in—I feel like a gerbil in a cage, running on its wheel. I want off so badly.

This is not to say I feel unloved; I don't. Everyone tells me all the time that I am loved. But really needed? No.

The whole routine reminds me so much of how I used to try to persuade Grandpa, at age 89, that our loving him was reason enough for his staying alive. I knew it wasn't enough for him, and I know it more now.

Without Bud, I think when I feel this way, I am nothing. Not alive, not feeling, not anything. I don't want to be here.

I had convinced myself that by now everything would be better. Most of the time it is, but these black despairing moods still come. I recognize that the best way to exorcise them is to write about them. Writing helps me acknowledge the complete selfishness of such thinking, the total disregard of the children's feelings and love. How could they ever explain such a thing to those nine grandchildren who try so hard to cheer me? They would all be afraid they had not done enough! No, I love them too much for that.

THE *E*IGHTH MONTH

Such a wailing wall! Why don't I write in this journal about all the happy times—the laughter, the noisy family gatherings, the sticky good-night kisses from the loveys padding their way to bed? I should write about the fun I have shopping with my children for bargains, the inside-the-family jokes, the outrageously funny things that my grandchildren say and do.

The warmth of friendship, those phone calls on gloomy rainy days, the drop-in friend who comes at just the right moment, the regular weekend visits that mean so much—these are the nourishment of my life. The days are full of activity, stimuli, love...things we all long for.

I have finally bought a puppy, and she is good for me. I get angry at her. She exasperates me. I laugh at her antics. She loves me and she is warm, her heart beating beneath my hand.

Josie absolutely demands my attention, stealing everything in sight just to plague me. But crawling under a table to rescue a lamb chop is better than sitting by myself staring at four walls.

Sensing another presence in the house takes away some of the emptiness. We have orgies of me telling Josie over and over how much I love her and need her, and does she love me? She answers with her deep black eyes and ecstatic wiggles.

Funny how I should need to say the words aloud.

I have read at least a hundred books these past few months but I hardly remember one. Of course, many were chosen to divert— murder mysteries and spy stories. What really worries me is my inability to concentrate still. I read about two pages and then have to rest a few moments. I almost feel as though the two years of Bud's illness, when I worried constantly, burned up my brain cells. Do other people experience what is happening to me now? Is it part of the grieving process or is it old age? Almost everyday I pick up a book, start it, realize it is vaguely familiar, check the end and sure enough—I read it last month!

THE NINTH MONTH

*S*urrounded by my warm, loving family I feel good. Surrounded by other people, not so good. I either talk too much, try too hard, or withdraw.

I saw a couple our age yesterday, holding hands walking down the street. I almost hated them, and had to look away. If I see a husband and wife, both healthy but obviously not happy, I feel real anger. How dare they waste life like that?

Society is so couple oriented. There is no place for a widow except on the fringe. Widowers are luckier; single men are always in demand. A widow—this widow, at least—feels like a second-class citizen, an outsider, someone people have to make a special effort to invite and include. I resent this, but at the same time I remember the part I played in the scenario before. I never remembered the single women either.

How to translate this into something more healthy, I'm not sure, but I keep trying. I find I am accepting all invitations eagerly and returning all. I try to invite someone for dinner or lunch at least once a week. Even though I'm out of practice and have had several near-disasters in cooking, I forge ahead. The guests are polite and the feeling of friendship along with the accomplishment is worth the effort.

So many other little things keep me going. Number one is the thought that every day I must achieve something positive, however small. Something creative is best, such as writing, knitting or sewing—anything I can look back on at the end of the day and say "I did it."

I keep busy. Too busy sometimes, and I have to force myself to pace my busyness. But just doing things and going places isn't the solution. There has to be that small, constructive something each day or I slide back into the slough. Sometimes lassitude smothers me. Everything becomes too much of an effort. Just to stay alive and

care about anything becomes over-whelming. *Forget the projects!* Then I need a push—from family, from friends, maybe even from a therapist or counselor; I don't know. I have to force myself to get up and out, and it isn't easy.

Most of the time, though, the sure-fire remedy for breaking a bad spell is to get out of the house. A walk downtown becomes a major outing. Other people and other scenes can avert a downslide for me. And to be honest, the walking

does me good. My feet may be tired but my mind is clearer.

Sometimes nothing works. Grief possesses me totally. I know now it's best to allow myself this feeling, and I cannot imagine it will ever go away. At least I'm not fighting the grief any more. Maybe it's getting easier.

THE TENTH MONTH

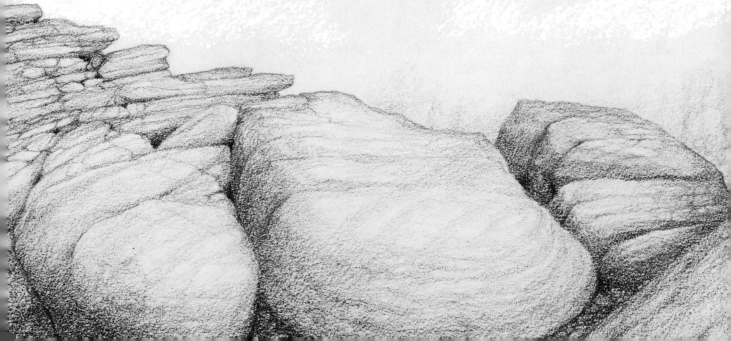

Whatever would I do without the children? I do hope I don't become a burden—a chore—to them. I must remember to ask for little, only what I have to have. And don't whine!

They said they had a discussion about me the other day. "She's improved," they decided. My question is "What was I like before this? Did they see in me the same things that I saw?"

"You're more flexible now," they say. I say I am only what I always was, but am adjusting to new situations. I who never drove alone before can now zip around the Beltway. I'm even thinking of driving to Indiana myself! I am gaining the confidence, out of necessity, I think, to be assertive with repairmen and salespeople.

Bud used to say, "Everyone should have something to look forward to...to plan for. Planning is half the fun." So I am going to figure out some places I can go out of town (mostly to see old friends) that will become my reward for trying hard. With good friends I don't feel like that half-person. My self-esteem returns.

A drastic change in scenery will be good for me. I find myself saying too often "I'll do that later." I must make myself do things now.

M. took me to lunch (with his wife's permission, of course) yesterday at the Four Seasons. I cannot express how important this was to me. Not because it was such a poshy place, but because someone thought I was worth taking there. We didn't flirt or anything, but he made me feel as if he were glad to be there with me. Two and a half hours...and with wine! I admit I am female enough still to find this important. I felt good for hours.

So many things are comforting, in a painful way. I closed the sale on our sailboat today. I like the young couple who bought it, thank goodness. He, particularly, was delighted to be buying it. As we were walking away from the bank he asked, "Would you care to see it?"

That was the last thing on earth I would do, and, swallowing tears, I thanked him, my nose turning that unavoidable red that comes when I try not to cry. He made an aborted attempt to pat my arm and said quietly, " I just want you to know something. When we first got the boat I found your husband's flip-flops tucked behind some equipment you had left for us. I felt terrible at first and wanted to throw them out, but I couldn't. Finally I looked at them and said, 'Hey, they stay. After all, this is his boat.''

I understand now why people attach so much importance to gravestones. We want a permanent record—something that others can see and think about and remember. I do so want people to know Bud. There are some things that no one can know as well as I did, or as well as the children did. But there are so many other parts of him—what he was and what he did—that should be remembered.

The grandchildren are making fun of me now with all my "stories," in a nice way, of course. I guess I have turned into the family reference book for anecdotes, but the telling does help me. Besides, I want them to remember their grandfather.

When I arrived home I went to a wedding reception—disaster. No backup system for arriving or leaving. That awful suspicion that people talk to me because they are sorry for me. Such an inferiority complex I have acquired! And no matter what anyone tells me, that's how I feel. So now I'll sit and remember the lunch with M.; then I'll feel good again.

Incidentally, when I told M. how the children were genuinely surprised at how tough I have become, he laughed. "I always knew you were," he insisted.

I am tough now. I know I can do anything I have to do. But much of the time, I don't want to, and that's different.

Oh wonder of wonders...I had a good dream last night, the first real one. Bud and I were sitting on a beach. He looked so tan and healthy and was smiling as he turned to me and said, "I'm not taking any more courses in anything. I know all I want to know."

He had that funny, special smile, and I reached out and we held hands. I actually could feel in my dream the warmth of his hand. I woke up truly happy for the first time in a year.

I had a letter today from someone who said that she, too, slept with an article of her husband's clothing. "Weird," she said, "but whatever gets you through the night!" I keep Bud's shirt close to me in the drawer now, just in case I need it. Sometimes I just take it out and hold it to my face. I wish it still smelled the good smell of him.

THE ELEVENTH MONTH

*M*uch of this journal seems to be a blues tune. I only seem to turn to it when I am ready to give up. You know what's the matter with me? I am spoiled rotten. I've already had everything I ever wanted in the world as far as material things are concerned. I've realized almost every dream—five children, the constant learning and seeing through travel, and most of all, the happiest 41 years of marriage anyone ever had. To have been loved as I was and to love as I did was a lifetime of happiness.

I had so much. Now nothing seems to live up to what I had. Such self-pity!

So...off to the busy-busy...the only answer.

After this last down period I have had a stretch of not sleeping. I wake up so frequently it hardly seems as if I sleep at all, although of course I do. Then from five to six a.m. I finally fall asleep—to dream my "release" dreams.

Three mornings in a row I have been furious because either Bud was ignoring me or had left me. I do release anger that he is gone this way, and I suppose that's good. But all the time in these dreams *there is the hope, the expectation that he will come back. That still leaves me frustrated, but less angry.*

I never quite appreciated the difficulty of people living alone until this morning when I slipped in the shower and almost had a catastrophe. My immediate thought was " Ye Gods! What if I'm found dead in the shower? How awful!"

Even suicide has its moments of black humor. I had discussed half jokingly with the children how I just couldn't

find an acceptable method. Slitting wrists is too gory, hanging traumatizes the person who finds you, and I have a feeling that if I jumped off a bridge I would automatically want to swim for shore. "I know," I finally said with a grim smile. "I'll just walk off into the sea some day."

The discussion was so macabre that I forgot all about it. But when two of the kids and I were lying on the beach the other day it all came back. Since the beach was completely deserted—not a soul but us—I had put on a disgraceful bikini suit that Bud bought for me once. The girls were asleep in the sand, so I went beach-combing. Up the shoreline was a huge coral head looming out of the shallow water. Without thinking, I scuffled out in the rippled pools on the far side, completely out of sight of the girls. They told me later that one sat up, looked for me, and in terror, shook her sister. "Wake up! Mother's gone and done it! She's walked into the sea!"

"Relax," said the calm and practical one. "It's low tide, and besides, Mother would never be caught dead in that bathing suit." She was absolutely right.

There are times now when I see the value of "groups" most clearly. I need to know if the memories I have will ever be good ones. Most of mine are still about Bud's last illness—the terrible sense of impending doom, the desperate attempt to stretch each moment, to make life last. The visual memories are all of him so thin, so brave, so determinedly cheerful. The few times he showed his true feelings are seared on my mind forever, yet I am glad we were so close he could share his thoughts.

To counteract this pain I talk a lot about the good times, the funny memories, even his faults, just so I can make him more real and blot out the agony of the very end.

To talk about this in a group would help, for I hesitate to discuss these things with the children unless they bring them up. Why make them as miserable as me? I confess I often do call them, and they urge me to talk. One doctor said to me, "What a support system you have in that family!"

Sometimes they sense when I have a down time and will all call on the same night. They say nothing about it, but immediately start telling me all their troubles: career crises, teenage children problems, financial woes, etc., all designed to make me feel absolutely necessary to them. I hang up feeling very needed...and totally overwhelmed. There isn't a thing I can do for any of them, but I certainly haven't time to think of myself!

I have begun working with a group which is starting a Hospice. After our family's experience, I know how valuable such help can be. I'm not anywhere near ready for "one-on-one" volunteering, but maybe I can help with the organizing. It's good for me to get out and around and do things with people.

Sometimes, though, I think it's a mistake to try to appear confident and "over the hump." Do people think I am cold? Do they know how I feel when I'm at the beach and keep seeing his long brown feet stretched out beside mine? Or even how I feel when I see a gas station where we stopped on a trip once? I stood next to a man at the newstand today who was wearing "Old Spice" shaving lotion and I almost burst into tears. The world is so full of reminders.

Every once in a while a blessed peace comes over me. I feel as though I am a whole, worthwhile person. I am still

ambivalent about this. How dare I?
I long for the grieving to be over, yet
I don't want to let it go. Will I be disloyal
if I step out as the new, whole me? Bud
was so sure I needed him to survive. So
was I. How dare I do so well without
him?

I can tell at gatherings and with my
Hospice work that people are thinking
of me, not as a widow, but as a person.
I gain a little confidence each day.

Part of that confidence, I guess, is
knowing what I can and cannot do. It's
occured to me more than once lately that
the dangers of living alone are very real.
That's why things like telephone

reassurance programs, where people call
old persons regularly to check on them,
are such a wonderful idea. I don't quite
qualify for that yet, but I'm aware of the
need. I've stopped cleaning out the
outside gutters from the step ladder;
I've bought a step-stool for inside work.

I had pneumonia this month at home
and we all panicked. The children called
every day. They wanted to take days off
from work to come take care of me.
Friends were wonderful—food, calls,
concern. But I am used to a physician
husband who diagnosed and cured me
(with occasional help, of course). Oh,
how I missed him these past weeks!

ONE YEAR

A year has passed. No, not true. 365 days have gone by, each one a mountain climbed. I did not dare write in this journal on the anniversary of Bud's death. I am such a practical person that I had been telling myself for weeks that it was only a date on the calendar. Not so.

The children, too, seem unable to let the day go by unmarked. I had phone calls, even flowers. Sentiment aside, there is disruption of my biorhythm, something entirely out of my control.

I am still referring to myself as Dr. Brooks' wife, not his widow. I went to a party last night with a male friend and he asked me if I ever thought of remarrying. "Who, me? Oh, no." He assured me no one should ever say never. Many wives who had happy first marriages welcome a second. "Not I," I stubbornly replied.

True, I'm lonely enough, and there are practical as well as emotional reasons. I desperately need someone to fix things: little things like the balky storm window, big things like the leaning fence, things he used to do. I weary of all the responsibility—the trash, the bills, the repairs, the paranoia of feeling cheated by repairmen.

I long for someone to be here, to comfort me, to make me feel loved. But to be bluntly honest, I'm a one-man woman. I'd take the marriage, but never the bed. No way can I imagine myself in someone else's arms, in anyone else's bed. Someday I might change my mind, but right now, it's not for me.

I'm beginning to see what the girls meant when they said I'm more flexible. What they really mean is I am making decisions often from the heart rather than the head. Last month on a trip to Canada to visit Penny I overheard a stewardess tell a little girl's grandfather that the airline couldn't take the girl on the flight. Landing was questionable, she said, because of a snow storm, and the child was being sent home un-accompanied. I impulsively offered to be responsible for her—so the little girl went along with me. I might never have done that if Bud had been alive. I would have thought of all the possibilities and dangers.

That's another thing: danger. Although not reckless, I seem impervious to death and danger. At least twice lately in near-miss accidents (I wasn't driving either time), I noticed that my heart never missed a beat. Are my senses dulled? Have I realized that there are worse things than death?

Maybe if my religious faith were more structured this past year would have been easier. While I respect and admire those with the solace of prayer, when it comes to religion I always seem to have more questions than answers. The only thing I do know is that sharing helps, whether it be with a journal, with fellow travelers or with God.

Maybe that's the most important part: the sharing. It's hard to believe I am still sitting here writing in this journal. I have actually survived a whole year. Surely if I could do it, anyone can. I am beginning to remember Bud now as he had been—strong, vibrant, funny and alive.

And yet...

It's not the passion I miss.
No need for fireworks;
I had it all
and loved the loving.

But nights in cold and single bed,
I yearn for what was purest gold:

The circling arms, the beating heart
beneath my head,
The warmth, the love, the safeness
there,
His breath feathering on my cheek,
His hand smoothing down my hair.

I'd sell my soul to Mephistopheles
For just one night
Encircled there.

I know that there is a world out there
full of people just like me. Some have
been alone all their lives, and the
solitude is much easier for them. But for
now, I will try to remember the joy and
learn to live with it...the grieving.

POSTSCRIPT

This is a testament to love and loss.
To withhold grief is destructive;
to release it, healing.
The writing of this book was my lifeline.
May the reading help your grieving time.
You are not alone.